The Realme Concept Phone Transformable Camera User Guide

Complete Manual with Step-by-Step Tips on Setting Up, Using, and Mastering the Smartphone-Camera Hybrid In NO-TIME. For BEGINNERS & SENIORS

RHODA DALY

Dedication

Dedicated to all those who embrace learning and technology with an open heart, and to those who help make the world a little bit easier for others—especially beginners and seniors—on their journey to mastering new skills.ok

Table of Contents

Introduction

1.1 Welcome to Your Realme Transformable Camera Experience

Congratulations on your purchase of the **Realme Concept Phone with Transformable Camera!** This innovative device bridges the gap between cutting-edge smartphone technology and professional-grade photography. Whether you're an avid photographer, a mobile enthusiast, or someone just looking to take better photos, this guide will help you unlock the full potential of your new device.

By combining a smartphone's convenience with the capabilities of a mirrorless camera, the Realme Concept Phone offers you a whole new world of creative possibilities. It's time to take your photography to the next level.

1.2 Why Choose Realme's Interchangeable Lens Concept Phone?

The Realme Concept Phone isn't just any smartphone – it's a game-changer. It stands out from other devices by allowing you to attach full-frame mirrorless lenses, turning your phone into a powerful camera system capable of capturing high-quality images usually reserved for professional cameras.

Here's why you should consider choosing the Realme Concept Phone:

- **Versatility:** Switch between lenses with ease, giving you flexibility in how you capture your world.

- **Professional Quality:** Achieve DSLR-like image quality, offering rich detail and vibrant colors.

- **Portability:** Take professional-grade photos without carrying heavy camera gear.

- **Innovative Design:** The transformable lens system makes photography more convenient and intuitive than   ever   before.

If you're looking for a smartphone that offers much more than the typical mobile photography experience, this is the device for you.

1.3 Key Features & Benefits

The Realme Concept Phone is packed with cutting-edge features that are sure to enhance your photography and smartphone experience. Here's what you can expect:

- **Interchangeable Lens System:** Attach professional lenses like a portrait or telephoto lens to your phone for versatile photography options.

- **Custom 1-Inch Sensor:** Capture stunning photos with great detail and clarity, even in low light conditions.

- **Professional Camera Settings:** Get full control over aperture, shutter speed, and focus for an elevated shooting   experience.

- **Sleek, Modern Design:** Enjoy the look and feel of a high-end device without the bulk of traditional cameras.

- **User-Friendly Interface:** Easily switch between modes and access all camera settings through an intuitive app.

With these features, the Realme Concept Phone ensures that you're equipped with everything you need for exceptional photography on the go.

1.4 Who This Guide is For

This guide is designed for anyone who wants to maximize their use of the **Realme Concept Phone with Transformable Camera.** Whether you are:

- A **beginner** just starting out in mobile photography.

- An **enthusiast** looking to enhance your creative skills.

- A **professional** photographer seeking a portable, high-quality solution.

- A **tech lover** excited about exploring new smartphone innovations.

No matter your level of expertise, this guide will provide you with easy-to-follow steps to make the most of your device's incredible features. From setting up your phone to mastering the camera system, we've got you covered.

Chapter 1: Unboxing and Getting Started

1.1 Opening the Box: What's Inside

When you open the box of your **Realme Concept Phone with Transformable Camera,** you'll find everything you need to start using your new device right away. Here's what's included:

- **Realme   Concept   Phone**
  Your brand-new smartphone featuring a sleek design and the innovative transformable camera system.

- **Camera   Lenses**
  Depending on the model, you may find lenses like a **portrait lens** or **telephoto lens** included in the package, giving you instant access to professional-level   photography.

- **Charging   Cable   and   Adapter**
  A high-speed USB-C cable and adapter to keep your device   charged   and   ready   to   go.

- **Protective   Case**
  A durable case to keep your phone safe and secure,

ensuring it's ready for all your photography adventures.

- **User   Manual**
  A quick-start guide that provides essential instructions on setting up and getting the most out of your Realme Concept Phone. This is the perfect companion to this detailed guide.

- **SIM   Card   Ejector   Tool**
  For easy installation of your SIM card.

- **Warranty   and   Safety   Information**
  Keep these documents handy for any future support   needs.

1.2 Device Overview: A Close Look at Your Realme Concept Phone

The **Realme Concept Phone with Transformable Camera** combines the best of smartphone technology with professional camera features. Here's a breakdown of the key components and design elements you'll find on the device:

- **Display:**
  The phone boasts a **6.7-inch AMOLED display** with vibrant colors and sharp resolution, perfect for both media consumption and editing your photos. The screen is edge-to-edge, providing a seamless visual experience.

- **Transformable Camera System:**
  The standout feature of this device is its **modular lens system.** On the back, you'll find the lens mount where you can attach different camera lenses, such as portrait and telephoto lenses, allowing you to switch between professional-grade photography setups with ease.

- **Camera Sensor:**
  The phone comes equipped with a **1-inch Sony sensor,** delivering excellent image quality even in low light conditions. This sensor enhances color accuracy and clarity, ensuring your photos stand out.

- **Power Button and Volume Controls:** The right side of the phone houses the power button, while the volume buttons are located just below it. Both are easily accessible and responsive for a smooth user experience.

- **USB-C Port and Speaker Grills:** The bottom of the phone includes a **USB-C charging port** and **stereo speakers** for crystal-clear sound. The speakers enhance the overall multimedia experience, whether you're listening to music or editing video.

- **SIM Card Slot:** On the left side, you'll find the **SIM card tray,** which is simple to access using the ejector tool provided. This allows for easy installation of your SIM card for mobile data and calls.

- **Fingerprint Sensor:** Integrated under the display, the **in-screen fingerprint sensor** ensures fast and secure unlocking of your phone. It's responsive and convenient, providing a seamless security feature.

- **Lens Attachment Mount:** The back of the phone features a special mount system that allows for easy attachment and detachment of camera lenses. This system is designed to securely hold your lenses while maintaining the phone's sleek design.

1.3 First Impressions: Setting Up the Phone

When you first hold your **Realme Concept Phone with Transformable Camera,** you'll immediately notice its sleek, premium feel. The device is lightweight, yet solid, with a smooth finish that gives it a modern, professional look. As you power on the phone for the first time, you'll be greeted with a clean, user-friendly interface that guides you through the setup process.

Here's how to get started:

1. **Powering On the Device:** Press and hold the **power button** located on the right side of the phone until the Realme logo appears on the screen. The display will come to life, and you'll be ready to begin.

2. **Language and Region Selection:** The first step in setting up your phone is selecting your preferred language and region. Simply tap the options on the screen to choose your settings.

3. **Wi-Fi Connection:** Connect your phone to a Wi-Fi network by selecting your network from the list of available

options. Enter your Wi-Fi password to connect and ensure you're connected to the internet for software updates and app downloads.

4. **Google Account Sign-In:** Sign in with your Google account to sync your contacts, apps, and data. If you don't have a Google account, you can create one during this step.

5. **Face Recognition or Fingerprint Setup:** Set up security features such as **face recognition** or **fingerprint scanning** for a quick and secure way to unlock your phone. This step is optional but recommended for added security.

6. **Software Updates:** Once your phone is connected to Wi-Fi, it may prompt you to download the latest software updates. These updates ensure that your device has the latest features and security patches.

7. **Finish Setup:** After completing the initial setup, you'll be directed to the home screen, ready to explore all

the features the Realme Concept Phone has to offer.

Your Realme Concept Phone is now ready to go. The setup process is simple and straightforward, taking just a few minutes to complete, so you can start enjoying your device right away.

1.4 Getting Connected: Basic Setup (Wi-Fi, Bluetooth, Camera Settings)

Now that your Realme Concept Phone is up and running, it's time to ensure it's properly connected to your network and accessories. Here's how to get connected:

Wi-Fi Setup:

- **Connecting to Wi-Fi:** Ensure you are connected to a stable Wi-Fi network. Go to **Settings** > **Wi-Fi** and select your network. Enter your password, and you're good to go! This is essential for downloading apps, software updates, and accessing cloud services.

- **Wi-Fi   Tips:**
  If you encounter issues connecting to Wi-Fi, try restarting your router or the phone. You can also toggle the Wi-Fi off and on from the quick settings menu   for   a   fresh   connection.

Bluetooth Setup:

- **Pairing   Devices:**
  To connect your **Bluetooth headphones, speakers, or other accessories**, go to **Settings** > **Bluetooth**, and toggle it on. The phone will search for nearby devices, and you can select the one you want to pair   with.

- **Managing   Connections:**
  Once paired, your devices will automatically reconnect when Bluetooth is enabled. If you need to manage or disconnect a device, just tap on its name   in   the   Bluetooth   settings   menu.

Camera Settings:

- **Launching   the   Camera   App:**
  Open the camera app by tapping the camera icon on the home screen. You'll be prompted to give the app permission to access the device's camera and storage. Grant these permissions to begin taking photos.

- **Initial   Camera   Setup:**
  The Realme Concept Phone comes with a variety of camera settings to choose from. To adjust settings:

  - Tap the gear icon in the top right of the camera app to access the **Camera Settings** menu.

  - Here, you can customize options like image quality, flash, grid lines, and more. Adjust these settings to match your photography style.

- **Lens   Setup:**
  Attach the lens you wish to use by aligning it with

the lens mount on the back of the phone. Once attached, the camera app will automatically detect the lens, and you'll be able to adjust the settings specific to that lens, such as aperture or focal length.

- **Camera   Modes:** Explore different camera modes by swiping through the options in the camera app. From **Portrait Mode** to **Manual Mode**, each setting is designed to give you full control over your shots.

Chapter 2

The Magic of the Transformable Camera

2.1 How the Transformable Camera Works

The **Realme Concept Phone with Transformable Camera** is a breakthrough device that combines the power of a smartphone with the versatility of professional-grade cameras. What sets it apart is its **transformable camera system,** which allows you to attach and use interchangeable lenses to capture stunning photos.

Here's how it works:

1. **Modular Camera System:** At the heart of the Realme Concept Phone is a modular camera system that can be customized with different lenses. Unlike traditional smartphones, which rely on fixed lenses, this phone lets you attach a variety of **professional-grade lenses,** such as **portrait, telephoto,** and **wide-angle** lenses. This gives you the ability to choose the best lens for any situation, whether you're

capturing close-ups, landscapes, or portraits.

2. Automatic Lens Detection: Once you attach a lens to the camera mount, the phone automatically detects it and adjusts the camera settings accordingly. This means you don't have to manually tweak settings when switching lenses; the camera app will optimize itself for the best performance based on the lens in use.

3. Enhanced Image Quality: The **1-inch Sony sensor** inside the Realme Concept Phone ensures that no matter which lens you attach, you'll get high-quality images with rich detail and color accuracy. The sensor is designed to handle a wide range of lighting conditions, from bright daylight to low-light environments, ensuring that your photos are crisp and clear every time.

4. **Seamless Integration with Smartphone Features:** The camera system is integrated directly into the phone's software, so you can switch between lenses and camera modes easily within the camera app. The interface is intuitive, and all of the controls for

lens adjustments, focus, and settings are right at your fingertips, making it easy to shoot like a pro.

2.2 Understanding the Lens Mount System: Attach and Detach with Ease

The **lens mount system** is a crucial part of the Realme Concept Phone's transformable camera, and it's designed for simplicity and ease of use. Here's a closer look at how it works:

1. **The Lens Mount Design:**
   Located on the back of the phone, the lens mount is a sleek, circular area where lenses attach and detach. The design ensures that the lenses lock into place securely without compromising the phone's slim, lightweight profile. The mount is durable and engineered to handle the weight and size of various professional-grade lenses, ensuring stability during use.

2. **Attaching the Lens:**
   To attach a lens, simply align the lens with the

mount on the back of the phone. The lens will click into place with a **quick and secure fit.** There are no complicated locking mechanisms; it's as simple as lining up the lens and twisting it gently into place. Once attached, the camera app will recognize the lens and adjust settings automatically for optimal performance.

3. Detaching   the   Lens: When you're ready to switch lenses, removing one is just as easy. To detach the lens, simply twist it counterclockwise, and it will release from the mount. The process is quick, clean, and smooth, allowing you to change lenses even while on the go. If you're switching between lenses quickly during a shoot, you'll appreciate how fast and hassle-free   this   process   is.

4. Compatibility   with   Multiple   Lenses: The lens mount is compatible with a variety of **Realme-approved lenses,** such as the **portrait lens** for sharp close-ups, the **telephoto lens** for zoomed-in shots, and the **wide-angle lens** for capturing expansive landscapes. Each lens is designed to offer professional-quality   results,   and   the   system

ensures that each lens attaches securely, giving you complete control over your shots.

5. **Protecting the Mount:**
The lens mount is built to last, but like any camera system, it's important to take care of it. Always ensure that the lens is properly secured and that the mount is clean from dust or debris before attaching a lens. This will help maintain the phone's performance and longevity.

2.3 Supported Lenses: Portrait, Telephoto, and More

The **Realme Concept Phone** is designed to provide a wide range of photographic possibilities through its **interchangeable lens system.** Here are some of the lenses that you can use to take your photography to the next level:

1. Portrait   Lens:

   The **portrait lens** is perfect for capturing stunning close-up shots, especially for people. It creates a beautiful **shallow depth of field,** making the subject stand out while softly blurring the background, a classic photography effect. Whether you're shooting portraits, pets, or any subject you want to highlight, this lens delivers professional-looking results.

2. Telephoto   Lens:

   The **telephoto lens** brings distant subjects up close with incredible detail, making it ideal for landscape photography, wildlife shots, and sports events. It allows you to zoom in without losing quality, ensuring your photos remain sharp and clear even from a distance. With this lens, you can take crisp, high-quality zoomed-in images that are often difficult to capture with a typical smartphone camera.

3. Wide-Angle   Lens:
   Capture more of your surroundings with the **wide-angle lens,** which expands the frame, allowing you to photograph sweeping landscapes or large groups of people. This lens is especially useful for architecture photography, travel shots, or interior photos, giving you the flexibility to include more in your shot without having to step back.

4. Macro   Lens   (Optional):
   The **macro lens** allows you to capture incredibly detailed close-up shots of small objects, such as flowers, insects, or textures. If you enjoy photographing the minute details of the world around you, the macro lens will open up a whole new   world   of   possibilities.

2.4 Interchanging Lenses: Step-by-Step Guide

Switching between lenses is simple, and the process is designed to be quick and easy, so you never miss a moment. Here's a step-by-step guide on how to interchange lenses:

1. **Step 1: Power On Your Phone and Open the Camera   App**
   Ensure that your **Realme Concept Phone** is powered on, and open the camera app. This ensures that the device is ready to detect any new lens   that   you   attach.

2. **Step 2: Choose the Lens You Want to Attach**
   Select the lens you want to use. Whether it's the **portrait, telephoto,** or **wide-angle lens,** make sure you have it ready to go. Align the lens with the lens mount   at   the   back   of   your   phone.

3. **Step   3:   Attach   the   Lens**
   Gently align the lens with the mount and twist it clockwise until it locks into place. The phone will automatically detect the lens and adjust its settings to match the capabilities of the lens. You should see the camera app reflect the new lens settings,

indicating   it's   ready   to   capture.

4. Step   4:   Start   Capturing   Photos
   Once the lens is securely attached, you can start using it for photography. You can also access lens-specific features in the camera app, such as aperture   or   focus   adjustments.

5. Step   5:   Detaching   the   Lens
   When you're ready to switch lenses, simply twist the lens counterclockwise to detach it. The process is quick, and the phone will remain in its ready state   for   the   next   lens.

6. Step   6:   Repeat   for   Other   Lenses
   If you want to switch lenses, repeat the above steps. The **Realme Concept Phone** ensures that each lens attaches securely, allowing for smooth transitions between different shooting styles and focal   lengths.

2.5 Key Features of the Camera System: Professional-grade Photography in Your Pocket

The **Realme Concept Phone with Transformable Camera** is packed with advanced features that make it a powerful tool for both amateur and professional photographers. Here are some key features that set it apart:

1. 1-Inch   Sony   Sensor:
   At the core of the camera system is a **1-inch Sony sensor** that captures high-resolution, detailed images. This sensor performs exceptionally well in low-light conditions, allowing you to take crisp, clear photos even when lighting isn't ideal. Whether you're indoors, at night, or in bright daylight, this sensor ensures excellent performance.

2. Advanced   Camera   Modes:
   The camera app includes a variety of modes to suit different   photography   needs:

   ○ **Pro Mode:** Offers full control over settings like **shutter speed, ISO, focus,** and **white** balance.

- o **Portrait Mode:** Optimizes settings for stunning portraits with background blur.

- o **Night Mode:** Enhances low-light performance, allowing you to take clearer pictures without the need for a flash.

- o **Macro Mode:** Lets you capture fine details with stunning clarity and focus.

3. **Manual Focus and Adjustable Aperture:** For those who want more control, the camera system provides **manual focus** and **adjustable aperture** options. These features allow you to fine-tune your shots, creating artistic effects like bokeh or achieving greater depth of field.

4. **Automatic Lens Detection:** When you attach a new lens to the mount, the phone automatically detects it and adjusts the camera settings to match. Whether you're using a portrait lens, telephoto lens, or wide-angle lens, the camera system is ready to give you the best

shot.

5. 4K   Video   Recording:
In addition to still images, the Realme Concept Phone supports **4K video recording** at 30fps. Whether you're capturing cinematic footage or everyday moments, you'll get smooth, high-quality video.

6. AI   Integration:
The camera system incorporates **AI enhancements**, which optimize image quality automatically. The AI adjusts color, sharpness, and exposure based on what you're shooting, ensuring vibrant   and   lifelike   results.

7. Stabilization   Technology:
To avoid blurry shots, the camera includes **optical image stabilization (OIS)**, which helps reduce camera shake when shooting photos or videos. This is especially useful when taking pictures at lower shutter speeds or while recording video on the   move.

Chapter 3

Mastering the Camera Interface

3.1 Navigating the Camera App: From Basic to Advanced Mode

The **Realme Concept Phone** comes with an intuitive camera app that is designed to cater to both beginners and advanced photographers. Whether you're taking a quick snapshot or diving into manual settings, the camera app is easy to navigate. Here's a guide to help you understand its features:

1. **Home Screen Overview:** Upon opening the camera app, you'll be greeted with a clean and straightforward interface. At the top, you'll find essential icons like flash settings, timer, and aspect ratio options. At the bottom, you'll see the shutter button, switch for front/back camera, and mode selection.

2. **Basic Mode (Auto Mode):** For quick, effortless shots, **Basic Mode** (also known as Auto Mode) is

perfect. In this mode, the camera app automatically adjusts settings such as exposure, focus, and white balance for optimal results. Simply point the camera at your subject and tap the shutter button to take the shot.

3. **Advanced Mode (Pro Mode):** If you're looking to take more control over your photos, **Pro Mode** is your go-to. In this mode, you have access to settings such as:

   o **Manual Focus** – Fine-tune the focus to ensure your subject is sharp.

   o **Shutter Speed** – Adjust the amount of time the shutter remains open, allowing you to control motion blur.

   o **ISO** – Control the camera's sensitivity to light, which helps in various lighting conditions.

   o **White Balance** – Adjust the color temperature to ensure true-to-life colors.

4. This mode is ideal for capturing photos with more creativity and precision, allowing you to experiment with various settings.

5. **Switching Between Modes:** To switch between modes, swipe left or right on the screen or tap the mode icon located at the bottom of the screen. You can easily switch from **Auto Mode** to **Pro Mode,** or explore other modes such as **Portrait Mode, Night Mode,** and **Macro Mode,** depending on the kind of shot you need.

6. Additional Modes:

   ○ **Portrait Mode:** Enhances depth of field for striking subject isolation, perfect for portraits.

   ○ **Night Mode:** Optimizes settings for low-light photography, ensuring clearer, brighter photos.

   ○ **Macro Mode:** Lets you capture extreme close-ups with incredible detail.

3.2 Customizing Settings: Aperture, Shutter Speed, and More

The Realme Concept Phone's camera app gives you complete control over the most important aspects of photography. Whether you want to adjust for lighting, motion, or creative effects, here's how you can fine-tune the camera settings:

1. **Aperture:**

   o The aperture controls how much light enters the camera, affecting depth of field and the exposure of your image. The larger the aperture (lower f-number), the more light the sensor receives, which is great for **low-light conditions** and creating **blurry backgrounds** (bokeh effect).

   o To adjust aperture, switch to **Pro Mode** and manually set the **f-stop** to control how much light enters the lens.

2. Shutter   Speed:

- ○ **Shutter speed** controls how long the camera's sensor is exposed to light. A **faster shutter speed** (e.g., 1/1000) will freeze motion, making it ideal for action shots, while a **slower shutter speed** (e.g., 1/30) allows for motion blur, which can create artistic effects such as **light trails** or **smooth waterfalls.**

- ○ In **Pro Mode,** you can adjust the shutter speed manually by tapping the shutter speed setting and rotating the dial to your desired speed. This feature is essential for creative photographers who want to control how movement is captured.

3. ISO:

- ○ **ISO** determines the sensitivity of the camera's sensor to light. A **higher ISO** allows you to take photos in low-light environments without a flash, but it can introduce **noise** (graininess) to the image. A **lower ISO** (e.g., 100) provides cleaner images but requires more   light.

○ To adjust ISO, tap the **ISO setting** in **Pro Mode** and set it according to the lighting conditions. For bright conditions, use a lower ISO (100-200), and for low-light or night scenes, increase the ISO (800-1600), keeping in mind the tradeoff between light and   noise.

4. White   Balance:

○ **White balance** helps to adjust the colors in your photos so they appear natural, especially in different lighting environments. Whether you're indoors under artificial light or outdoors in daylight, adjusting the white balance ensures that whites appear truly white and colors are accurate.

○ In **Pro Mode,** you can adjust the white balance to match your environment. Tap the **WB icon** and select from various presets (Daylight, Tungsten, Fluorescent, etc.) or manually adjust the temperature for precise color   control.

5. Focus:

  ○ In **Pro Mode,** you can adjust the **focus manually** to ensure that your subject is sharp and clear. This is particularly useful when you want to emphasize a specific area of your frame, such as a macro subject or a portrait with   a   blurry   background.

3.3 Switching Between Lens Systems: Maximizing the Camera's Full Potential

One of the standout features of the **Realme Concept Phone** is its **interchangeable lens system.** Switching between lenses opens up a world of creative possibilities. Here's how to maximize your camera's full potential by switching lenses:

1. **Understanding Lens Compatibility:** The Realme Concept Phone supports a variety of lenses that attach to the mount on the back of the device.

These lenses include:

- Portrait Lens for professional-looking depth and subject isolation.

- Telephoto Lens for long-distance zoom with clear details.

- Wide-Angle Lens for capturing expansive landscapes or group shots.

- Macro Lens for extreme close-up photography.

2. **Attaching a New Lens:** To switch lenses, gently twist the current lens counterclockwise to detach it from the mount. Align the new lens with the mount, then twist it clockwise until it locks securely into place. The camera will automatically detect the new lens and adjust the settings for optimal performance.

3. **Automatic Adjustments for New Lenses:** Once a new lens is attached, the camera app will detect it and make automatic adjustments to settings such

as focal length and aperture. This means you don't have to manually tweak settings each time you change lenses – the app will handle it for you.

4. **Switching Lenses During a Shoot:** The Realme Concept Phone makes it easy to switch lenses even during a shoot, so you can quickly adapt to changing conditions. Whether you're shooting portraits in one moment and switching to landscape shots in the next, the phone allows for seamless   transitions.

5. **Creative Possibilities:** The ability to switch between lenses and customize settings means you can shoot a variety of scenes with the best lens for the job. Use the **portrait lens** for stunning close-ups, the **telephoto lens** for capturing distant subjects, or the **wide-angle lens** for grand landscapes. Each lens opens up unique creative opportunities, giving you more control over how you capture the world around you.

3.4 Manual Focus and Exposure Control

To take your photography to the next level, **Manual Focus** and **Exposure Control** are essential features that provide you with full creative control. These settings allow you to fine-tune your shots to achieve exactly the results you want, whether you're shooting in challenging lighting conditions or aiming for a specific artistic effect.

Manual Focus:

- **Why Use Manual Focus?** Manual focus is ideal when you want to have precise control over what part of your image is sharp. It's particularly useful for macro photography, portraits, or when shooting in low light where autofocus may struggle to lock onto the correct subject.

- **How to Adjust Focus:** In **Pro Mode,** you can adjust the focus manually by sliding the focus control on the screen. Rotate the control left or right to change the focus distance, ensuring the subject you want to highlight is crisp and clear. You'll see the focus shift as you adjust, helping you to pinpoint the perfect   focus   for   your   shot.

- **Tips for Manual Focus:**

  - Use **focus peaking** (a feature available in Pro Mode) to see exactly what parts of the image are in focus. The areas in focus will appear highlighted in a bright color on your screen.

  - For **macro shots,** use manual focus to ensure that the tiny details of your subject are captured sharply without the camera misfocusing.

Exposure Control:

- **What is Exposure?**
  Exposure refers to the amount of light that hits the camera sensor. It affects the brightness and detail in your image. A correct exposure ensures that the photo isn't too dark (underexposed) or too bright (overexposed), allowing you to capture every detail of your scene.

- **How to Adjust Exposure:** In **Pro Mode**, you can control exposure by adjusting the **shutter speed** and **ISO.** Shutter speed controls how long the camera's sensor is exposed to light, while ISO determines the sensor's sensitivity to light.

  - **Shutter Speed:** Use a slower shutter speed for more light in dark scenes or faster shutter speeds for motion shots (e.g., sports).

  - **ISO:** Increase ISO in low-light conditions for brighter photos, but be mindful that higher ISO values can introduce noise.

- **Tips for Exposure:**

  - For bright daylight scenes, keep ISO low and use a fast shutter speed.

  - In low-light situations, increase ISO and lower the shutter speed to capture more light, but watch out for motion blur if the subject is moving.

○ Use the **exposure compensation** slider to adjust the overall brightness of your photo without altering other settings.

3.5 Using the Camera for Different Scenarios: Portraits, Landscapes, and More

The Realme Concept Phone's **transformable camera system** and **customizable settings** make it an excellent choice for a variety of photography scenarios. Whether you're shooting portraits, landscapes, or everyday moments, the camera has the tools to help you get the best shot.

Portrait Photography:

- **Lens Choice:** Use the **portrait lens** for crisp, detailed images with a beautifully blurred background (bokeh effect). This lens is perfect for isolating your subject and creating stunning, professional-looking portraits.

- **Settings** **Tips:**

- In **Pro Mode,** adjust the **aperture** to a wider setting (lower f-stop) to create a shallow depth of field, blurring the background and making the subject stand out.

- Use **manual focus** to ensure the subject's eyes are sharp and clear.

- **Lighting:**

  - Ensure good lighting on the subject's face. Natural light is ideal for portraits, but if shooting indoors, use soft artificial light to avoid harsh shadows.

Landscape Photography:

- **Lens Choice:** For wide scenes, use the **wide-angle lens.** It captures more of the environment in a single shot, making it perfect for expansive landscapes, cityscapes, or large group photos.

- **Settings** Tips:

○ In **Pro Mode,** adjust **ISO** to a low setting (100-200) for clearer, sharper images with less noise. Use a slower **shutter speed** to allow more light in, especially during dawn or dusk.

○ Ensure the entire scene is in focus by using a smaller **aperture** (higher f-stop), which increases the depth of field and keeps both foreground and background sharp.

- **Composition:**

  ○ Follow the **rule of thirds** by placing your horizon along the lower third of the frame. This will add balance and interest to your shot.

Low-Light and Night Photography:

- **Lens Choice:** The **telephoto lens** can help capture distant lights or subjects at night, while the **wide-angle lens** works well for capturing cityscapes and starry   skies.

- Settings   Tips:

  - In **Night Mode,** the phone automatically adjusts settings to maximize exposure in dark conditions. You can also adjust **ISO** and **shutter speed** manually in **Pro Mode** to avoid noise and ensure crisp images.

  - Use a **tripod** or stable surface to avoid motion blur when using slower shutter speeds.

Action and Sports Photography:

- **Lens Choice:** The **telephoto lens** is ideal for action shots, allowing you to capture fast-moving subjects without losing detail.

- Settings   Tips:

  - Use a fast **shutter speed** to freeze motion and ensure the subject is sharp. A setting of 1/1000 or faster is often ideal for sports or high-speed action.

- Keep **ISO** at a higher setting to compensate for the faster shutter speed, ensuring that your photo remains bright.

Macro Photography:

- **Lens Choice:** For capturing tiny details like flowers, insects, or textures, use the **macro lens**.

- **Settings** Tips:

  - Use **manual focus** to precisely focus on small objects. This ensures that intricate details, such as the texture of a leaf or the patterns on an insect's wings, are captured sharply.

  - A smaller **aperture** (higher f-stop) helps to keep the entire subject in focus when shooting at close distances.

Chapter 4

Photography Tips & Tricks

4.1 Best Practices for Handheld Shooting with Attached Lenses

Shooting handheld with attached lenses, especially professional-grade ones, requires a steady hand and proper technique to achieve sharp, clear images. Here are some best practices to ensure your shots are steady and your photos look as professional as possible:

1. **Use Both Hands:**
   Always hold your **Realme Concept Phone** with both hands for better stability. Keep your fingers on the sides of the phone and grip the lens to prevent any unwanted shaking. This also allows you to manage the lens more securely when switching between attachments.

2. **Proper Hand Positioning:**
   Hold the phone close to your body to minimize movement. Tuck your elbows into your sides, creating a tripod-like effect with your arms. This

adds extra stability, especially when using heavier lenses.

3. Elbow   Brace:
   For extra stability, lean your elbows against your torso or a stable surface like a table or wall. This technique minimizes any slight hand movements, helping   you   capture   sharper   images.

4. Hold   Your   Breath:
   Before taking the shot, gently exhale and hold your breath for a second. This eliminates any slight movement caused by breathing, which can blur your photo, especially at slower shutter speeds.

5. Use the Camera's Timer or Remote Shutter:
   If you have the option, set a timer or use a remote shutter to avoid shaking the camera when pressing the shutter button. This is especially useful when using   slower   shutter   speeds.

6. Use   Image   Stabilization:
   If your Realme Concept Phone or the lens you are using has built-in **optical image stabilization (OIS)**, make sure it is enabled. This helps to counteract

any small hand movements and improve image sharpness.

4.2 Achieving Stable Shots: Tips for Clear, Sharp Images

To achieve clear and sharp images, stability is key. When shooting handheld or in challenging conditions, there are several strategies you can employ to ensure your photos come out crisp and free from motion blur:

1. Use Faster Shutter Speeds: The faster your shutter speed, the less likely you are to capture any unintended movement. For handheld shooting, aim for a shutter speed of at least 1/500 or faster to freeze motion and avoid blur, especially if you're photographing moving subjects.

2. Increase ISO in Low-Light Conditions: In low-light settings, increasing the ISO can help you capture brighter photos at faster shutter speeds, reducing the risk of motion blur. However, be mindful of noise – try to keep the ISO as low as

possible while still achieving a properly exposed image.

3. **Stabilize Your Body and Camera:** As mentioned earlier, use both hands to hold the phone securely. Keep your elbows tucked in, and avoid unnecessary body movements. Consider standing with your feet shoulder-width apart for a firm base, or if possible, use a tripod to achieve maximum stability.

4. **Use the Grid Feature:** Enable the **grid lines** in the camera settings to help align your shot and improve composition. The grid will also assist in keeping your horizon level, which can prevent slight tilting that may make your images appear unsteady.

5. **Lock Focus and Exposure:** When focusing on a subject, tap and hold to lock the focus and exposure. This ensures that your phone doesn't re-adjust while you take the shot, providing a more stable and consistent image.

6. **Utilize Image Stabilization:** Ensure that the **optical image stabilization (OIS)** feature is activated on both your Realme Concept Phone and the lens. This minimizes shake and helps you achieve sharper images, particularly when shooting at slower shutter speeds or zoomed-in shots.

4.3 Lighting and Composition: Creating Stunning Visuals with Every Click

Good lighting and strong composition are the foundation of great photography. By mastering these elements, you can elevate your images and create stunning visuals with every shot. Here's how to make the most of lighting and composition:

Lighting Tips:

1. **Use Natural Light:** Natural light is often the most flattering and versatile. When shooting portraits, try to position your subject near a window or in open shade for soft, even lighting. Avoid direct sunlight, as it can

create harsh shadows and overexposed highlights.

2. Golden Hour Lighting:
For the most flattering light, aim to shoot during the **golden hour**—the hour after sunrise or before sunset. The light is soft, warm, and directional, creating a beautiful glow on your subjects.

3. Avoid Overexposure:
Be cautious of bright light sources like the sun, as they can easily lead to overexposure. Use the **exposure compensation** feature in your camera settings to adjust the brightness of your images.

4. Artificial Light:
If shooting indoors or at night, consider using **soft artificial lighting**. Avoid using harsh overhead lights; instead, try **diffusing light** through lamps or softboxes. Positioning the light at a 45-degree angle to the subject can create a natural-looking effect.

5. Side and Backlighting:
For dramatic effect, experiment with **side lighting** (where the light hits your subject from the side) or

backlighting (where the light source is behind the subject). These lighting techniques can create stunning contrasts and highlight textures.

Composition Tips:

1. **Rule of Thirds:**
   The **rule of thirds** is a compositional guideline that helps to create balanced and dynamic images. Imagine dividing your frame into a 3x3 grid. Position your subject along one of the vertical or horizontal lines, or place it at one of the intersection points. This creates more visual interest and prevents your subject from being placed in the center, which can make photos appear static.

2. **Leading Lines:**
   Use natural lines in your scene (such as roads, fences, or buildings) to lead the viewer's eye toward the main subject. This technique creates a sense of depth and movement in your photos.

3. **Framing the Subject:**
   Use elements within your environment to frame

your subject. For example, you could use doorways, windows, or tree branches to create a natural frame around your subject, drawing attention   to   it.

4. **Symmetry   and   Patterns:**
Look for symmetry and repeating patterns in your surroundings. Symmetry can add harmony to your images, while patterns can create visual interest. Use the gridlines on your camera to help line up symmetrical   shots.

5. **Fill   the   Frame:**
Don't be afraid to get close to your subject. Filling the frame with your subject eliminates distractions and ensures that the viewer's attention is focused on   what   matters   most   in   the   shot.

4.4 Tips for Mobile Photography Enthusiasts: Achieving DSLR-like Results

While smartphones, like the **Realme Concept Phone**, are not typically equipped with the large sensors and lenses of a DSLR, they can still produce stunning, DSLR-like results with the right techniques. Here are some tips to help you achieve professional-level photos:

1. **Use Manual Mode (Pro Mode):** Take full control of your shots by switching to **Pro Mode**. Adjust **shutter speed, ISO,** and **focus** manually to tailor the exposure and look of your images. These settings allow you to replicate the control you would have with a DSLR, giving you the ability to fine-tune your photos for maximum quality.

2. **Work with Depth of Field:** One of the hallmarks of DSLR photography is the ability to control depth of field, creating a sharp subject with a beautifully blurred background (bokeh effect). The **portrait lens** on your Realme Concept Phone is designed for this effect, but you can further enhance it by adjusting the **aperture** in

Pro Mode. The lower the f-stop (e.g., f/1.8), the more pronounced the blur in the background.

3. Use a **Tripod** or **Stabilizer:** To get sharp, steady shots, especially in low light, use a **tripod** or a **gimbal stabilizer.** These tools help eliminate camera shake, especially at slower shutter speeds. Even with the **optical image stabilization (OIS)** on your phone, a tripod will ensure a steady shot, which is crucial for long exposures or capturing fine details.

4. Shoot in **RAW:** When shooting in **Pro Mode,** consider enabling **RAW capture** (if available). RAW files retain more image data than JPEGs, giving you more flexibility in post-processing to adjust exposure, color balance, and sharpness without losing quality. This is a key feature that DSLR photographers use to get the most out of their images.

5. Leverage the **Right** **Lighting:** DSLR photographers rely heavily on good lighting, and mobile photographers can do the same. **Natural light** is often the best, especially

during the **golden hour** (shortly after sunrise or before sunset). If you're shooting indoors, use **diffused lighting** from windows or softboxes to mimic the soft lighting you'd get with a DSLR.

6. Focus on Composition:
DSLR shots often excel because of their **composition.** Apply the **rule of thirds**, use leading lines, and focus on symmetry in your photos. Don't rely solely on the camera's auto mode—take your time to frame the shot and think about how each element in the scene contributes to the overall image.

7. Post-Processing:
After capturing your images, use **photo editing apps** to bring your photos closer to the DSLR quality you're aiming for. Apps like **Adobe Lightroom, Snapseed,** or **VSCO** allow you to adjust contrast, sharpness, and color balance, and even apply presets that give your photos a professional, cinematic feel.

4.5 Taking Full Advantage of the Sensor's Capabilities

The 1-inch Sony sensor in your **Realme Concept Phone** is a key component that allows you to achieve professional-quality photos, even though it's in a smartphone. To make the most of this powerful sensor, here are several tips to help you capture stunning images:

1. **Leverage the Larger Sensor for Low-Light Performance:** One of the biggest advantages of a larger sensor is its ability to capture more light, which is essential for **low-light photography.** In **low-light conditions,** the larger 1-inch sensor allows you to take clearer, sharper photos with less noise compared to smaller sensors typically found in smartphones. Keep **ISO** as low as possible to prevent grain, and use a **slower shutter speed** to allow more light to hit the sensor.

2. **Achieve Better Dynamic Range:** A larger sensor has better **dynamic range,** which means it can capture more details in both bright highlights and dark shadows. To take advantage of this, use **exposure bracketing** or adjust the **exposure**

compensation to avoid clipping highlights or losing detail in shadows. This will ensure that your images have a more balanced and natural look.

3. **Create Stunning Depth of Field Effects:** The 1-inch **sensor** allows for a more pronounced **depth of field** effect. By using the **portrait lens** and adjusting the **aperture,** you can create beautiful **bokeh** (background blur) while keeping your subject in sharp focus. This is a hallmark of DSLR photography, and with the larger sensor, you can achieve similar effects without the bulk of a traditional   camera.

4. **Use the Sensor's High Resolution for Detailed Shots:** The larger sensor allows for high-resolution images that retain detail even when zoomed in. When taking landscape or architectural photos, make sure to use the highest possible resolution to preserve all the intricate details in your shot. The sensor's resolution will also allow you to crop photos without losing too much quality, giving you more   flexibility   in   post-editing.

5. **Maximize Image Quality with the Right Lens:** Pairing the 1-inch sensor with the right lens is crucial for maximizing image quality. Whether you're using the **telephoto lens** for distant shots or the **wide-angle lens** for landscapes, the sensor will capture the full potential of the lens, producing sharper images with better color accuracy.

6. **Post-Processing Flexibility:** Because the 1-inch **sensor** captures more data, your images will have more information to work with in post-processing. This allows you to make adjustments to the exposure, contrast, and color balance without degrading the image quality. You can make significant edits, such as enhancing shadows or brightening highlights, without sacrificing clarity or   detail.

7. **Shoot in RAW for Maximum Flexibility:** As mentioned in the previous section, shooting in **RAW format** preserves the full potential of the 1-inch sensor. RAW files contain more color information and dynamic range, allowing for more detailed edits. If you're aiming for professional-grade results, RAW is the preferred format, as it

gives you the most control over your final image.

Chapter 5

Troubleshooting and Maintenance

5.1 Common Problems and How to Fix Them

While the **Realme Concept Phone with Transformable Camera** is designed to deliver a seamless experience, you may encounter a few issues during use. Here's a guide to some common problems and their solutions:

1. Lens Not Detected

- **Problem:** Sometimes the phone may not recognize a newly attached lens.

- **Solution:**

  - **Reattach the Lens:** Ensure that the lens is securely attached to the mount. Gently twist the lens clockwise to make sure it locks in place.

  - **Restart the Camera App:** Close the camera app and reopen it to reset the system.

- ○ **Reboot the Phone:** If the lens is still not detected, restart the phone to ensure the system refreshes.

2. Blurry Photos

- **Problem:** Your photos come out blurry even after focusing.

- **Solution:**

  - ○ **Check Lens Stability:** Make sure the lens is securely attached to the mount and isn't loose.

  - ○ **Use Faster Shutter Speed:** If you're shooting handheld, increase the shutter speed to freeze motion and reduce camera shake.

  - ○ **Enable Image Stabilization (OIS):** Ensure that optical image stabilization is turned on if your lens supports it.

○ **Manual Focus:** In **Pro Mode,** adjust the focus manually to ensure the subject is sharp.

3. Poor Low-Light Performance

- **Problem:** Photos in low-light conditions appear noisy or grainy.

- **Solution:**

  ○ **Increase ISO:** In **Pro Mode,** increase the ISO for better exposure, but be mindful of noise. Aim for a balance between ISO and shutter speed to get clearer results.

  ○ **Use Night Mode:** If available, use **Night Mode,** which automatically adjusts settings for better low-light performance.

  ○ **Use a Tripod:** To avoid motion blur, stabilize your phone by using a tripod or a stable surface when shooting in low light.

4. Camera App Freezing or Crashing

- **Problem:** The camera app stops working or crashes unexpectedly.

- **Solution:**

    ○ **Force Close the Camera App:** Go to the settings, open the app manager, and force close the camera app before restarting it.

    ○ **Update the Camera App:** Make sure that your camera app is up to date by checking for software updates in the **App Store.**

    ○ **Clear Cache:** Clear the cache of the camera app through the app settings to remove any temporary files that may be causing issues.

5. Overexposed or Underexposed Photos

- **Problem:** Your photos are either too bright (overexposed) or too dark (underexposed).

- Solution:

  ○ **Adjust Exposure:** Use the **exposure compensation** slider to adjust the brightness of your image.

  ○ **Use Manual Mode:** In **Pro Mode,** adjust the **shutter speed** and **ISO** manually to control the exposure.

  ○ **Check the Lighting:** Ensure that the subject is adequately lit, and avoid direct sunlight or overly bright light sources.

5.2 Managing Lens Compatibility and Performance

The **Realme Concept Phone** supports a range of **interchangeable lenses** that provide flexibility and allow you to capture professional-quality images. However, to get the best performance and avoid compatibility issues, follow these guidelines:

1. Check Lens Compatibility:

- **Official Lenses:** Always use **Realme-approved lenses** to ensure compatibility. Using third-party lenses or non-compatible lenses can affect image quality, cause focusing issues, or prevent the camera from functioning properly.

- **Lens Mounting System:** The lenses are designed to fit securely on the **lens mount** at the back of the phone. Ensure that each lens matches the system and attaches correctly without force.

- **Firmware Updates:** Keep your device's firmware updated to ensure compatibility with new lenses or future lens features.

2. Lens Performance:

- **Aperture and Focal Length:** Different lenses will offer varying focal lengths and aperture sizes. Be mindful of the **depth of field** and **bokeh effect** each lens produces. For instance, **portrait lenses** will give you a shallow depth of field, while **wide-angle**

lenses allow you to capture more in a single shot.

- **Lens-Specific Settings:** The phone will automatically detect and adjust settings when a new lens is attached, but always double-check settings in **Pro Mode** to ensure the right focus and exposure adjustments are in place for the lens you're using.

3. Switching Between Lenses:

- **Avoid Frequent Switching in Extreme Conditions:** While switching lenses is designed to be quick and easy, try to avoid doing so in dusty or harsh environments to prevent dirt or debris from entering the lens mount.

- **Proper Lens Handling:** When switching lenses, always handle them by the edges and avoid touching the glass to prevent smudges, dust, or scratches. Store unused lenses in a safe, clean environment.

4. Lens Care and Maintenance:

- **Regular Cleaning:** Clean your lenses after each use to ensure optimal performance. Dirt or smudges on the lens can degrade image quality.

- **Use Lens Caps:** When not in use, always cover your lenses with their **lens caps** to protect them from dust and scratches.

5.3 Cleaning Your Lens and Camera System for Longevity

Proper care and maintenance of your camera and lenses are essential for maintaining performance and extending the life of your Realme Concept Phone. Here's how to clean your device's camera system effectively:

1. Cleaning the Lens:

- **Use a Microfiber Cloth:** The best way to clean your lens is by using a **soft microfiber cloth.** Avoid using tissues, paper towels, or your fingers, as these can scratch the lens or leave behind fibers.

- **Gentle Wipe:** Gently wipe the lens in a circular motion to remove fingerprints, dust, or smudges. For more stubborn spots, lightly dampen the cloth with water or a lens-safe cleaning solution, but avoid using excessive moisture.

- **Avoid Harsh Chemicals:** Never use harsh cleaning chemicals or household cleaners, as these can damage the lens coating and affect image quality.

2. Cleaning the Lens Mount:

- **Keep the Mount Free of Dust:** Over time, dust or dirt can accumulate around the lens mount, potentially interfering with lens attachment or detection. Use a **soft brush** or a **lens blower** to remove any particles around the mount.

- **Inspect the Mount Regularly:** Check the lens mount for any signs of wear or damage. Ensure that it's free from dust and debris, especially when switching between lenses.

3. Cleaning the Camera's Sensor (if applicable):

- If your phone allows direct access to the **camera sensor,** use a sensor cleaning kit designed for smartphones. If not, it's best to leave sensor cleaning to professionals. Cleaning the sensor improperly can lead to permanent damage.

- **Professional Cleaning:** If you notice dirt or spots in your photos that can't be removed with a lens wipe, consider having the camera system professionally cleaned.

4. Cleaning the Display:

- **Use a Soft Cloth:** Clean your phone's screen regularly with a soft, dry microfiber cloth to remove fingerprints and smudges. For a more thorough cleaning, slightly dampen the cloth with water and wipe gently.

- **Screen Protector:** Consider using a **screen protector** to keep the display safe from scratches, dust, and smudges.

5. Storage and Protection:

- **Store Lenses Safely:** When not in use, store your lenses in a **lens pouch** or **case** to protect them from scratches and dust. Ensure that they are kept in a clean, dry environment.

- **Use a Case for Your Phone:** Protect the entire device with a sturdy case to prevent accidental drops and exposure to dust.

5.4 Maximizing Battery Life with Heavy Photography Usage

When using the **Realme Concept Phone** for heavy photography, especially during long shoots or when using power-hungry features like the camera and high-resolution lenses, battery life can be a concern. Here are some practical tips to help you maximize battery life without compromising your photography experience:

1. Adjust Screen Brightness:

- **Lower Screen Brightness:** The display is one of the most power-consuming components of your phone. Lowering the brightness or enabling **Auto-brightness** will help conserve power, especially when you're not in direct sunlight.

2. Use Battery Saver Mode:

- **Enable Battery Saver:** When you're in a pinch and need to extend battery life, enable **Battery Saver Mode** in the settings. This reduces background processes and limits non-essential functions, allowing you to keep shooting longer.

3. Turn Off Unnecessary Features:

- **Disable Wi-Fi, Bluetooth, and GPS:** If you're not using Wi-Fi, Bluetooth, or GPS for your photography session, turn these features off to conserve power.

- **Limit Background Apps:** Close any apps running in the background that you don't need during your photo shoot. Apps like messaging or social media can drain your battery even if you're not actively using them.

4. Manage Camera Settings:

- **Lower Resolution for Quick Shots:** If you're taking photos quickly and don't need full resolution, you can reduce the camera resolution in the settings to save power. This will also result in smaller file sizes, which is helpful when you're on the go.

5. Use Airplane Mode:

- **Enable Airplane Mode:** If you're in an area where you don't need cellular data or Wi-Fi, turn on

Airplane Mode. This can prevent your phone from constantly searching for a signal, saving battery life.

6. Keep the Lens Cool:

- **Avoid Overheating:** Long photography sessions, especially with high-performance lenses, can cause your phone to overheat and use more battery. If the phone feels warm, give it a break for a few minutes to cool down. This will help prevent rapid battery   drain.

7. Use an External Power Bank:

- **Carry a Portable Charger:** If you're planning on shooting for extended periods, consider carrying a **portable power bank.** This can be particularly useful during long shoots or travel when you might not have access to a charging outlet.

8. Update to the Latest Software:

- **Optimized Battery Usage:** Ensure that you have the latest software updates, as manufacturers often include battery optimizations in new firmware releases.

5.5 Software Updates and Keeping Your Camera Up to Date

Keeping your **Realme Concept Phone**'s software up to date is essential not just for performance improvements but also for ensuring that your camera system remains fully optimized. Here's why software updates matter and how to manage them:

1. Why Software Updates Matter for Your Camera:

- **Bug Fixes and Performance Enhancements:** Software updates often include fixes for known bugs and camera performance enhancements, ensuring smoother operations and more accurate camera functions.

- **New Features and Camera Modes:** Updates can introduce new features, such as additional camera modes, improved lens functionality, or enhancements to **Pro Mode.** By regularly updating, you ensure that your camera system stays up-to-date with the latest technological advances.

- **Compatibility with New Lenses:** As Realme releases new lenses or lens updates, software updates are important to ensure full compatibility and smooth integration with your device. The camera app will recognize new lenses and optimize settings automatically, so updating is critical for a seamless   experience.

2. How to Check for Software Updates:

- **Automatic Updates:** Most of the time, your **Realme Concept Phone** will notify you when a new update is available. If you have **automatic updates** enabled, the phone will download and install the updates as soon as they're available, ensuring that your system   is   always   current.

- **Manual Updates:** To check for updates manually, follow these steps:

  1. Go to **Settings** > **Software Updates.**

  2. If a new update is available, you'll see a prompt to **download** and **install** it.

  3. Make sure your phone is connected to Wi-Fi and plugged into a charger if necessary, as updates can consume a significant amount of data and battery life.

3. Updating the Camera App:

- **Camera App Updates:** Your phone's camera app may also receive separate updates through the **App Store** or **Realme's software update system.** These updates may include new features or improvements specific to the camera.

- **Update Frequency:** To ensure that you are always using the latest version, check for updates regularly in the **App Store** or the **Realme Store.**

4. Managing Camera Settings after Updates:

- **Recalibrate Settings:** After a major update, it's a good idea to recalibrate your **camera settings.** Check **focus modes, exposure settings,** and **lens compatibility** to make sure everything is working as expected.

- **Explore New Features:** Take time to explore new features that might have been introduced in the update, such as improved **AI functionality, additional manual controls,** or **new shooting modes.**

5. Backup Your Photos Before Updating:

- **Data Backup:** While software updates are generally safe, it's always a good idea to **backup your photos** and other important data to a cloud service or external storage before updating. This ensures that your images are secure in case of any unexpected issues during the update process.

Chapter 6

Advanced Features for Professional Photographers

6.1 Unlocking the Full Potential of the Realme Camera System

The **Realme Concept Phone** is equipped with advanced features that, when fully utilized, allow you to achieve professional-level photography results. To unlock its full potential, follow these key steps:

1. Master Manual Mode (Pro Mode):

- **Control Over Settings: Pro Mode** gives you complete control over essential camera settings like **shutter speed, ISO, white balance,** and **focus.** Mastering these settings allows you to capture images with precise exposure, focus, and motion control.

- **Shutter Speed:** Adjust the shutter speed to freeze fast action or create smooth motion blur for artistic effects.

- **ISO:** Use a lower ISO in bright conditions and a higher ISO in low-light situations, keeping an eye on noise levels.

- **Focus:** Use manual focus to ensure that your subject is as sharp as possible, especially when working with macro shots or portraits.

2. Utilize the Interchangeable Lenses:

- Take advantage of the **transformable camera system** by switching between the **portrait lens, telephoto lens,** and **wide-angle lens** depending on your shooting needs.

- Each lens is designed for specific types of photography—use the **portrait lens** for beautiful subject isolation, the **telephoto lens** for zoomed-in shots, and the **wide-angle lens** for expansive scenes.

3. Explore Advanced Camera Modes:

- **Portrait Mode:** Enhance your portrait photography with professional-level subject isolation and bokeh effects.

- **Night Mode:** This mode is great for low-light conditions, allowing you to capture brighter, clearer images without introducing noise.

- **Macro Mode:** Get up close to capture tiny details with remarkable clarity and sharpness.

- **AI Features:** Enable AI enhancements for automatically optimized shots, especially when shooting landscapes or portraits.

4. Experiment with Raw Image Capture:

- Shooting in **RAW** format gives you more flexibility in post-processing, as it retains more detail and color data than standard JPEG images. If you're looking to take your editing to the next level, RAW files will allow you to adjust exposure, white balance, and other elements without degrading the quality of the image.

5. Leverage the Camera's 1-Inch Sensor:

- The **1-inch Sony sensor** is designed for excellent low-light performance and high dynamic range. To make the most of this sensor, shoot in conditions that allow you to take advantage of its strengths, such as during **golden hour** or in darker settings where other sensors may struggle.

6. Keep Software Updated:

- Regular **software updates** will improve camera performance and often add new features. Make sure to install updates to ensure that your camera is running at peak performance.

By mastering the manual controls and experimenting with different modes and lenses, you'll be able to unlock the full creative potential of your **Realme Concept Phone** and achieve impressive, professional-grade results.

6.2 Connecting External Accessories for an Elevated Experience

To further elevate your mobile photography experience, consider connecting **external accessories** that enhance the functionality of the **Realme Concept Phone.** These tools can help you capture high-quality photos, video, and improve stability, giving you more control over your shots.

1. External Lenses:

- **Wide-Angle or Fisheye Lenses:** While the Realme Concept Phone's interchangeable lens system provides a variety of options, external lenses like **fisheye** or **super-wide-angle** lenses can further enhance your ability to capture unique shots.

- **Macro Lenses:** For extreme close-ups beyond what the built-in macro lens offers, external **macro lenses** can provide additional magnification for detailed shots of small objects.

2. Tripods and Stabilizers:

- **Tripods:** A **tripod** is essential for steady shots, particularly when using slower shutter speeds or when you need to shoot in low-light conditions without blur. Many **portable tripods** are lightweight and easy to carry, perfect for travel and landscape   photography.

- **Gimbal Stabilizers:** For **video** shooting, a **gimbal stabilizer** will help eliminate shaky footage, ensuring smooth, cinematic shots. This is particularly useful for action shots or while walking   around   while   filming.

3. External Microphones:

- **Improved Audio Quality:** If you plan to record **video** on your phone, using an **external microphone** can significantly improve sound quality. Built-in microphones on smartphones often pick up background noise, but an external mic, like a **lavalier mic** or **shotgun mic**, will provide clearer,   more   professional   audio.

4. Lighting Gear:

- **LED Lights:** Portable LED lights or **ring lights** can be used for better **portrait photography, video recording,** or when shooting in dim environments. These lights are adjustable and can help you control the direction, intensity, and color of light in your scene.

- **Softboxes and Diffusers:** These accessories help soften and diffuse light, reducing harsh shadows and creating a more natural look for your photos.

5. Remote Shutter Release:

- **Wireless Shutter:** A **remote shutter release** allows you to take photos without touching your phone, which is ideal for avoiding any camera shake, especially in low-light settings or when using slower shutter speeds. This is also a great accessory for **group** **shots** or **selfies.**

6. Power Bank:

- For extended photography or video shoots, bring along a **portable power bank** to keep your phone charged. This is particularly useful when you're out for long shoots and don't have access to a charger.

6.3 Integrating with Professional Editing Software

While the **Realme Concept Phone**'s camera system offers powerful features, **post-processing** is an essential step for many photographers and videographers. Integrating your mobile photography with professional editing software allows you to fine-tune your images and videos to achieve the highest quality. Here's how you can integrate your photos with professional software:

1. Editing Photos with Adobe Lightroom:

- **RAW Files:** If you've captured photos in **RAW** format, **Adobe Lightroom** is one of the best tools for editing these images. Lightroom allows you to adjust exposure, white balance, highlights, shadows, and fine-tune color grading with precision.

- **Presets:** Lightroom also offers a wide variety of **presets** that can give your photos a professional, polished look with just a few clicks. You can create your own custom presets or use pre-built ones to achieve consistent results.

2. Using Photoshop for Advanced Edits:

- For more complex edits, such as removing objects, advanced retouching, or blending multiple images, **Adobe Photoshop** offers powerful tools. You can import your photos from the **Realme Concept Phone** into Photoshop for detailed editing, layer manipulation, and more.

3. Mobile Editing Apps:

- If you prefer editing directly on your phone, several **mobile apps** offer professional-level editing tools:

  - **Snapseed:** Snapseed is a free and user-friendly app with a wide array of features like **healing,** **lens** **blur,** and **filters.**

- VSCO: VSCO is known for its clean interface and excellent set of **presets** and filters, allowing for easy edits with a professional finish.

- **Afterlight:** Afterlight offers both powerful editing tools and creative filters, making it an excellent choice for editing photos directly on your phone.

4. Video Editing with Adobe Premiere Rush or Final Cut Pro:

- For video work, you can integrate your footage with professional editing software like **Adobe Premiere Rush** or **Final Cut Pro** (on Mac). These programs allow you to edit your videos, apply color corrections, and even add effects and transitions to create polished, cinematic content.

5. Cloud Storage and Integration:

- Using **cloud storage services** like **Google Photos, Adobe Creative Cloud,** or **Dropbox** allows you to easily sync your photos and videos across devices, making it easier to edit them on both your phone and computer. This integration ensures you have access to your work anytime and anywhere.

6. Collaborate and Share with Professional Communities:

- Once you've edited your photos or videos, share them with the **photography community** or clients. Services like **Behance** (for Adobe users) or **500px** allow photographers to showcase their work, get feedback, and collaborate with other professionals.

6.4 Using the Camera for Video Production: Tips for Filmmakers

The **Realme Concept Phone** is not just a powerful tool for still photography; it's also an excellent choice for **video production**. With its advanced camera system, interchangeable lenses, and manual controls, this phone can be a valuable asset for filmmakers. Here are some tips for using your phone's camera to create professional-quality video:

1. Stabilize Your Shots:

- **Use a Tripod or Gimbal:** To ensure smooth, stable footage, always use a **tripod** or **gimbal stabilizer** when shooting video. A **gimbal** helps eliminate shake, giving your video a cinematic look, especially when you're moving with the camera.

- **Practice Steady Handheld Shooting:** If you don't have access to a stabilizer, use **proper handheld shooting techniques:** keep your elbows close to your body, use both hands, and walk with your knees slightly bent to absorb motion.

2. Frame Your Shots Using the Rule of Thirds:

- When setting up your shots, use the **rule of thirds** to create balanced and dynamic compositions. Enable the **gridlines** on your camera to help you align the subject and elements in the scene according to the grid. This technique will enhance the storytelling aspect of your video.

3. Control Exposure and Focus:

- **Manual Focus:** Use the **manual focus** feature in **Pro Mode** to ensure that your subject is always in sharp focus, especially for interviews or detailed shots.

- **Adjust Exposure:** Set the **shutter speed** and **ISO** manually to get the perfect exposure. A good rule of thumb for video is to set the **shutter speed** to **double your frame rate**. For example, if you're shooting at **30fps**, set your shutter speed to **1/60**.

- **Lock Exposure and Focus:** Once you've set the right exposure and focus, lock them in so the camera doesn't automatically adjust during the shot.

4. Use the Right Frame Rate:

- For most cinematic looks, shoot in **24fps** (frames per second), as it mimics traditional film. For smoother motion, such as in action scenes, you can increase the frame rate to **60fps** or higher. If you want to create slow-motion effects, you can go for **120fps** or even **240fps** (if supported by your phone).

5. Utilize Lighting for Professional-Looking Footage:

- **Natural Light:** Always make use of natural light when possible. Position your subject near windows or shoot during the **golden hour** (early morning or late afternoon) for soft, flattering lighting.

- **Artificial Lighting:** For consistent lighting indoors, use soft **LED lights** or **ring lights**. Avoid harsh overhead lighting, as it can create unwanted shadows. For more creative lighting, consider using **backlighting** or **side lighting** to create mood and depth in your scenes.

6. Use External Microphones for Better Audio:

- **Clear Audio:** Audio is crucial in video production. Built-in microphones often pick up ambient noise, so consider using an **external microphone** for clearer, more professional audio. A **lavalier mic** (clip-on mic) or a **shotgun microphone** will provide much better sound quality, especially in interviews or noisy environments.

7. Post-Production:

- After filming, **edit your video** using software like **Adobe Premiere Rush** or **Final Cut Pro**. These tools will allow you to adjust color grading, fine-tune audio, and make your video stand out with transitions, effects, and stabilization features.

6.5 Leveraging RAW Image Capture for Maximum Control

While the **Realme Concept Phone** provides excellent image quality out of the box, shooting in **RAW format** offers significant advantages for those who want maximum control over their photos. RAW files retain all the data captured by the camera's sensor, which means you have more flexibility in editing. Here's how you can leverage **RAW image capture** for better results:

1. What is RAW and Why Use It?

- **RAW Files vs JPEG:** Unlike **JPEG**, which compresses and processes the image to save space, **RAW files** retain all the image data. This means they are larger in size, but they give you much more control over **exposure, white balance, sharpness,** and **color grading** during post-processing.

- **More Dynamic Range:** Since RAW files contain more data, they have a greater **dynamic range,** allowing you to recover more detail in both highlights and shadows without degrading image quality.

2. When to Shoot in RAW:

- **Low-Light Conditions:** When shooting in low light, RAW files will allow you to recover more detail from dark areas and reduce noise in post-processing.

- **High Dynamic Range Scenes:** RAW is ideal for scenes with high contrast, such as landscapes or cityscapes, where there's a significant difference between the lightest and darkest parts of the image.

- **Portrait Photography:** For portraits, RAW allows you to fine-tune skin tones and adjust lighting without losing image quality.

3. How to Shoot in RAW:

- **Enable RAW Mode:** In the **camera settings**, enable RAW capture. This may be located under the **Pro Mode** or **advanced settings** options. Some phones also offer **RAW + JPEG** options, where both the compressed JPEG and the unprocessed RAW file are saved.

- **Check Storage Space:** RAW files take up more space than JPEGs, so ensure that you have enough

storage on your phone or an external device to store your photos.

4. Post-Processing RAW Files:

- **Use Professional Software:** To unlock the full potential of RAW files, use professional editing software like **Adobe Lightroom** or **Capture One**. These programs allow you to make detailed adjustments to:

    - **Exposure:** Brighten or darken your photo without degrading quality.

    - **White Balance:** Correct color temperature and tint to ensure accurate colors.

    - **Sharpness and Detail:** Enhance the fine details without introducing noise.

    - **Noise Reduction:** Remove unwanted noise, especially in low-light photos.

- **Non-Destructive Editing:** RAW files allow for **non-destructive editing**, meaning you can make adjustments without altering the original file. You can always revert to the original settings, giving you full flexibility to experiment with different edits.

5. Benefits of RAW for Professional Work:

- **Professional Quality:** If you're using the **Realme Concept Phone** for professional work or high-quality prints, shooting in RAW ensures that your final images maintain the highest possible quality.

- **Creative Control:** With RAW, you can experiment with various edits, from changing the mood of a scene through color grading to fine-tuning the sharpness and detail of your shots. This level of control is essential for professional photographers who need to get the perfect result from every shot.

Chapter 7

Realme's Ecosystem and Your Photography Journey

7.1 Seamless Integration with Other Realme Devices

One of the standout features of the **Realme Concept Phone** is its ability to seamlessly integrate with other **Realme devices**, creating a cohesive and enhanced ecosystem. Here's how to maximize the connectivity and benefits when using your phone alongside other Realme products:

1. Syncing with Realme Tablets and Laptops:

- **Multi-Screen Collaboration:** If you have a **Realme tablet** or **laptop**, you can use the **Realme Link** app to sync your devices. This allows you to easily transfer files, photos, and videos between your phone and tablet or laptop, improving workflow and   saving   time.

- **Unified Notifications:** With **Realme's ecosystem,** notifications from your phone can be mirrored on your tablet or laptop, allowing you to stay up to date even when you're away from your phone.

2. Realme Smartwatch Integration:

- **Health and Fitness Tracking:** The **Realme Concept Phone** works seamlessly with **Realme smartwatches** to track your fitness and health data. You can view your heart rate, steps, and other health metrics directly on your phone.

- **Remote Camera Control:** Use your **Realme smartwatch** to remotely control the camera on your phone. This is particularly useful when taking group photos or long-exposure shots where you want to avoid shaking the camera.

3. Realme Buds and Audio Gear:

- **Perfect Audio Pairing:** Connect your **Realme wireless earbuds** or **headphones** to the phone for superior audio quality during media consumption or video recording. The **Realme Concept Phone** supports high-definition audio codecs for a richer sound experience.

- **Low-Latency Mode for Video Production:** If you're recording videos or gaming, you can use **Realme Buds** that support **low-latency audio**, ensuring that the sound stays in sync with the video.

4. Realme Smart Home Devices:

- **Smart Home Control:** The **Realme Concept Phone** can act as a hub for controlling your **Realme smart home devices** like lights, speakers, and security cameras through the **Realme Link** app. You can automate routines, adjust settings, and monitor your home directly from your phone.

By integrating the **Realme Concept Phone** with other Realme devices, you can enjoy a seamless, interconnected experience that enhances productivity, entertainment, and convenience.

7.2 Sharing and Collaborating with the Realme Community

One of the most exciting aspects of the **Realme Concept Phone** is the ability to share your photography and collaborate with the growing **Realme community**. Whether you're looking for inspiration, feedback, or want to showcase your work, here's how to engage with others:

1. Join the Realme Community:

- **Realme Forums:** The **Realme Community Forum** is a space where users can exchange tips, share photography techniques, and discuss the latest Realme products. You can join photography challenges, interact with like-minded enthusiasts, and learn from more experienced users.

- **Social Media Groups:** Follow **Realme's official social media accounts** and engage with other photographers by using relevant hashtags like **#RealmePhotography** or **#RealmePhotographyChallenge**. Share your images, tag Realme, and get involved with the larger   photography   community.

2. Participate in Photography Challenges:

- **Monthly Themes:** Realme regularly hosts photography challenges with themes that encourage creativity, such as **nature photography, night photography,** or **portrait photography.** Winning entries often receive recognition and rewards, such as exclusive Realme products or feature spots on Realme's social media platforms.

- **User Submissions:** Realme actively features user-submitted photos on their official channels, giving photographers a platform to showcase their skills. Participating in challenges is a great way to get your   work   noticed.

3. Collaborative Projects with Other Creators:

- **Collaborate with Fellow Photographers:** Realme's ecosystem makes it easy to collaborate with other creators. You can share and collaborate on projects through cloud storage, and even co-create content for social media or promotional campaigns.

- **Realme Creators Program:** The **Realme Creators Program** is designed to support photographers and content creators by providing them with resources, tools, and opportunities to showcase their work to a wider audience.

4. Share Photos with Cloud Services:

- **Instant Sharing:** With the **Realme Concept Phone,** you can instantly share your photos with friends, family, or social media followers. Directly upload your images to platforms like **Instagram, Flickr,** or **5oopx** to gain exposure and connect with other photographers.

Being part of the **Realme community** allows you to engage with fellow photographers, learn new techniques, and get valuable feedback on your work, creating an inspiring and supportive environment for your photography journey.

7.3 Cloud Services and Storage for Your Photos

As a mobile photographer, having reliable storage options for your images is crucial, especially when working with high-resolution RAW files or extensive video footage. Here's how to make the most of cloud services to store, organize, and access your photos from anywhere:

1. Realme Cloud Services:

- **Realme Cloud Storage:** Realme offers cloud storage options that allow you to back up your photos and videos seamlessly. With **Realme Cloud,** you can store your images in a secure and easily accessible space, ensuring you never lose important content.

- **Auto-Syncing:** Enable **auto-sync** to automatically upload your photos and videos to the cloud as soon as they're captured. This helps you maintain a backup of your content in real-time.

2. Google Photos Integration:

- **Google Photos Backup:** If you prefer using Google's platform, the **Realme Concept Phone** works flawlessly with **Google Photos** for cloud storage. Set up **automatic backup** to store all your images and videos, and enjoy unlimited cloud storage for photos in **high-quality resolution**.

- **Access Anywhere:** With **Google Photos**, you can access your photos from any device—whether it's your phone, tablet, or computer. Google's AI also helps you organize and find your photos by subjects, locations, or keywords, making it easier to locate specific images.

3. Adobe Creative Cloud:

- **For Professional Editing:** If you're a professional photographer, **Adobe Creative Cloud** integration allows you to store your RAW images and access them directly from applications like **Adobe Lightroom** and **Photoshop**. With cloud storage, you can edit your images across devices and ensure your work is always up-to-date.

- **Sync Across Devices:** With **Adobe's cloud services,** you can start editing on your **Realme Concept Phone** and continue on your laptop or desktop, maintaining consistency in your workflow.

4. Dropbox and Other Cloud Storage Services:

- **File Storage and Sharing:** You can also use other cloud services like **Dropbox, OneDrive,** or **iCloud** to store, share, and organize your photos. These platforms offer **secure file-sharing** options, so you can easily send high-resolution photos to clients or collaborators.

5. Local Storage for RAW Files:

- **External Storage:** If you're shooting in **RAW format,** which requires more storage space, it's a good idea to use an **external hard drive** or **SD card reader** for additional storage. You can transfer your RAW files from the phone to an external device to prevent running out of space on your phone.

7.4 Joining Photography Challenges and Competitions

Engaging in **photography challenges** and **competitions** is an excellent way to test your skills, gain recognition, and connect with other photographers. The **Realme Concept Phone** offers the perfect platform for capturing stunning images that you can submit to various photography contests and challenges. Here's how you can get involved:

1. Participate in Realme's Photography Challenges:

- **Monthly Themes:** Realme regularly hosts **photography challenges** with specific themes such as **portrait photography, landscapes, night photography,** or **creative compositions.** These challenges are a great way to practice different photography styles and showcase your creativity.

- **Winning Prizes:** Winning or participating in these challenges often comes with rewards such as **Realme products, exclusive features on Realme's official channels,** or **exposure on social media.** It's an excellent opportunity to gain recognition and connect with fellow enthusiasts.

2. Explore External Competitions:

- **Global Competitions:** Many global photography competitions, such as the **National Geographic Photo Contest** or the **Sony World Photography Awards,** accept mobile photography entries. With the **Realme Concept Phone's** advanced camera system, you can compete with traditional DSLR and mirrorless camera users.

- **Specialized Contests:** Look for competitions specifically for mobile photography, such as those hosted by **Mobile Photography Awards** or **Instagram photo contests.** These platforms allow mobile photographers to compete and earn recognition based on their skills and creativity.

3. Build Your Brand and Exposure:

- **Social Media Sharing:** Sharing your contest entries on platforms like **Instagram** or **Flickr,** tagged with the appropriate hashtags (e.g., #RealmePhotography), increases the chances of getting noticed by a broader audience. It's also a great way to engage with potential followers, brands, and other creators.

- **Engage in Feedback and Growth:** Participating in challenges often opens the door for constructive feedback from peers and judges. This helps you grow as a photographer by learning what works and what doesn't, and refining your craft.

7.5 Building Your Photography Portfolio Using Your Realme Concept Phone

A **portfolio** is a key tool for any photographer looking to establish themselves professionally, and your **Realme Concept Phone** can be an essential part of building that portfolio. Here's how you can use your phone to create a strong, standout photography portfolio:

1. Capture High-Quality Images:

- **Leverage Advanced Camera Features:** Take full advantage of the **Realme Concept Phone's** advanced features like **interchangeable lenses, Pro Mode,** and **RAW image capture** to produce high-quality photos that will impress potential clients or collaborators. Ensure each shot is thoughtfully composed and edited for maximum impact.

- **Diverse Shot Selection:** Include a variety of shots in your portfolio, such as **portraits, landscapes, macro photography,** and **night photography.** Showing versatility demonstrates your ability to adapt to different environments and subject matter.

2. Organize Your Portfolio by Genre:

- **Categorize Your Work:** Organize your portfolio into sections based on your style or genre, such as **portrait photography, commercial work, travel photography,** or **event photography.** This makes it easier for clients to navigate and helps highlight your range of skills.

- **Include High-Resolution Images:** Ensure your images are of high resolution for clients or galleries to see the detail and quality of your work. When creating your portfolio, consider displaying your images in **RAW format** or **high-resolution JPEGs** for   maximum   clarity.

3. Showcase Your Best Work:

- **Select Your Top Shots:** Curate your portfolio to showcase only your best work. Choose images that reflect your creative vision, technical ability, and storytelling skills. Less is more – you don't need to show everything you've shot, just the pieces that truly   represent   your   unique   style.

- **Tell a Story:** Where possible, aim to tell a story with your photos. A well-constructed series or theme will showcase your ability to think cohesively and create a visual narrative.

4. Create an Online Portfolio:

- **Portfolio Websites:** Consider creating a website or using platforms like **Adobe Portfolio, Behance,** or **Squarespace** to host your portfolio. These platforms offer customizable templates, and you can easily upload images, categorize them, and even   sell   your   work.

- **Social Media Presence:** In addition to your main portfolio site, create an **Instagram** or **Flickr** account dedicated to your photography. These platforms are great for building a following, connecting with other photographers, and showcasing your latest work.

5. Professional Touches in Post-Processing:

- **Editing for Consistency:** After capturing your photos, use professional editing software like **Adobe Lightroom** or **Snapseed** to polish your images. Edit for consistent color grading, exposure, and composition to ensure your portfolio has a cohesive look and feel.

- **RAW Files for Editing Flexibility:** When editing, start with **RAW files** to retain all the original data from your shots, allowing for more flexibility in adjusting settings such as exposure, white balance, and sharpness without losing quality.

6. Share Your Portfolio and Network:

- **Send to Potential Clients:** Once your portfolio is ready, share it with potential clients, brands, or agencies that align with your style. Include a personal message or cover letter that explains your creative vision, and how your work aligns with their   needs.

- **Collaborate and Connect:** Connect with other photographers, creative agencies, or brands on platforms like **LinkedIn, Instagram,** and **500px** to expand your network. Often, opportunities come through collaboration and personal connections.

Chapter 8

Comparison with Traditional Cameras and Other Smartphones

8.1 How the Realme Concept Stacks Up Against DSLR and Mirrorless Systems

The **Realme Concept Phone** with its **transformable camera system** is a revolutionary step in mobile photography, but how does it compare to traditional **DSLR** and **mirrorless** cameras? While smartphones like the Realme Concept Phone are not quite at the level of high-end professional camera systems, they offer unique advantages in terms of portability, flexibility, and ease of use. Here's a breakdown of how the Realme Concept Phone stacks up:

1. Image Quality:

- **DSLR/Mirrorless:** DSLR and mirrorless cameras are equipped with large **full-frame** or **APS-C sensors,** which are much bigger than the sensors in smartphones. These larger sensors capture more light and produce superior image quality, especially in low-light conditions. They also offer a wider dynamic range and the ability to achieve a more pronounced **depth of field** for bokeh effects.

- **Realme Concept Phone:** The **Realme Concept Phone** uses a **1-inch Sony sensor**, which is larger than typical smartphone sensors and provides excellent low-light performance. While it may not match the size of a full-frame sensor, it offers a notable improvement over traditional smartphone cameras. The phone also benefits from the ability to swap out lenses, further improving versatility.

2. Lenses and Flexibility:

- **DSLR/Mirrorless:** One of the primary advantages of **DSLR** and **mirrorless cameras** is their ability to use a wide range of **interchangeable lenses**, such as wide-angle, telephoto, and macro lenses, allowing for greater creative control and specialized shots.

- **Realme Concept Phone:** The **Realme Concept Phone** offers a similar advantage with its **modular lens system.** Users can easily attach lenses such as **portrait, telephoto,** and **wide-angle** lenses, giving them greater flexibility for different shooting scenarios. However, while it's versatile, the lens selection for smartphones is not as vast as what's available for traditional cameras.

3. Autofocus and Speed:

- **DSLR/Mirrorless:** These cameras typically have **fast autofocus systems** with features like **phase detection** or **contrast-detection,** which are excellent for tracking moving subjects, making them ideal for sports or wildlife photography.

- **Realme Concept Phone:** While the **Realme Concept Phone** does have **AI-enhanced autofocus** and manual focusing options, it may not be as fast or precise as the **autofocus systems** in professional cameras. However, its **transformable lens system** offers manual focus controls, giving the user more creative freedom in certain shooting situations.

4. Portability:

- **DSLR/Mirrorless:** While these cameras provide superior image quality, they tend to be bulky and require multiple lenses and accessories for different types of shots.

- **Realme Concept Phone:** The **Realme Concept Phone** is incredibly portable and lightweight, allowing you to take professional-level photos without the bulk of traditional camera gear. This makes it a great option for travelers or everyday users who want to carry their camera in their pocket.

5. Cost:

- **DSLR/Mirrorless:** High-quality DSLR or mirrorless cameras, along with lenses and accessories, can be quite expensive, often running into the thousands of dollars.

- **Realme Concept Phone:** While the **Realme Concept Phone** may not provide the same level of image quality as a professional camera, it offers a much more affordable option for those who want versatility and high-quality images without breaking   the   bank.

8.2 Comparing Performance: Realme vs Other Premium Smartphones

The **Realme Concept Phone** is a high-end device that promises to push the boundaries of mobile photography. However, how does it compare with other premium smartphones on the market, such as those from **Apple, Samsung**, and **Google**? Here's a comparison of the **Realme Concept Phone's** performance:

1. Camera System:

- **Realme Concept Phone:** Equipped with a **1-inch Sony sensor** and the ability to attach various lenses (such as **portrait, telephoto,** and **wide-angle**), the **Realme Concept Phone** offers a versatile and high-quality camera system that rivals some of the best in   mobile   photography.

- **Apple iPhone 14 Pro:** Known for its **ProRAW** and **ProRes** video capabilities, the iPhone features a powerful **48MP main sensor** and **Deep Fusion** technology for improved detail. While it doesn't have interchangeable lenses, it offers excellent **AI-enhanced photography** and **video capabilities.**

- **Samsung Galaxy S23 Ultra:** With its **200MP camera** and multiple **zoom lenses** (up to **10x optical zoom**), Samsung's flagship excels in capturing detailed shots, especially in zoomed-in and high-resolution situations. It also features advanced **AI-enhancements** for both photography and video.

- **Google Pixel 7 Pro:** Google's **Pixel** devices are renowned for their **computational photography** capabilities, with features like **Night Sight** for low-light shooting, **Super Res Zoom**, and **Real Tone** for accurate skin tones. It focuses more on software than hardware, but the results are excellent.

2. Lenses and Versatility:

- **Realme Concept Phone:** With its **transformable lens system**, the **Realme Concept Phone** offers true versatility, allowing users to swap between different lenses for various effects and perspectives.

- **Other Premium Smartphones:** Most other premium smartphones come with fixed **multi-lens systems** (wide, ultra-wide, and telephoto), but none offer the same modularity as the **Realme Concept Phone.** While the lenses on flagship devices like the **iPhone 14 Pro** and **Samsung Galaxy S23 Ultra** are top-notch, they don't offer the same level of customization or lens swapping.

3. AI and Software Enhancements:

- **Realme Concept Phone:** The **Realme Concept Phone** incorporates **AI-enhanced features** such as scene recognition and automatic settings adjustments, ensuring users get the best shot possible. The **Pro Mode** also allows full manual control.

- **Apple and Google:** Both **Apple** and **Google** rely heavily on **AI and computational photography.** Apple's **Deep Fusion** and **Google's HDR+** ensure high-quality results in all lighting conditions. While the **Realme Concept Phone** offers manual controls, it's more tailored toward users who want greater creative flexibility.

- **Samsung Galaxy S23 Ultra:** Samsung has heavily integrated **AI features,** especially in their **night photography** and **zooming capabilities,** providing excellent results in low-light and long-distance shots.

4. Video Recording:

- **Realme Concept Phone:** The **Realme Concept Phone** supports **4K video recording** at 30fps and utilizes its modular lenses for cinematic-style shots. It can be a great tool for mobile filmmakers.

- **Other Premium Smartphones:** The **iPhone 14 Pro** and **Samsung Galaxy S23 Ultra** offer **4K and 8K video recording** with excellent stabilization, ProRes, and 120fps at 4K, providing filmmakers with top-tier video performance. **Google Pixel 7 Pro** excels in **video stabilization** and low-light video quality but doesn't offer the same range of recording options as Samsung or Apple.

8.3 The Future of Photography: Why the Realme Concept Phone Is a Game-Changer

The **Realme Concept Phone** is not just a smartphone with impressive camera specs—it represents the future of mobile photography. By combining advanced hardware with cutting-edge software, it's paving the way for the next generation of mobile imaging. Here's why the **Realme Concept Phone** is a game-changer:

1. Modular Lens System:

- **Interchangeable Lenses:** The ability to swap lenses like a **mirrorless or DSLR camera** is something that hasn't been fully explored by other smartphone brands. The **Realme Concept Phone** is one of the first to offer this level of flexibility in a mobile device, allowing users to attach **portrait lenses, telephoto lenses,** and **wide-angle lenses** for professional-grade shots.

- **Creativity Unlocked:** This innovation opens up endless creative possibilities for photographers. The ability to change lenses allows for more diverse types of shots, making the **Realme Concept Phone** a versatile tool for both casual and professional   photographers.

2. Advanced AI and Computational Photography:

- **AI Integration:** The phone's **AI-powered** features enable automatic scene detection, ensuring optimal settings for various scenarios. As computational photography continues to evolve, the **Realme Concept Phone** is at the forefront of this transformation, using AI to enhance not just still images, but also **video** and **low-light photography.**

- **Real-Time Adjustments:** AI adjustments happen in real-time, making it easy for users to capture stunning shots without having to manually tweak every setting, while still offering **Pro Mode** for those who want more control.

3. 1-Inch Sensor:

- **Improved Low-Light Performance:** The **1-inch sensor** is a step up from typical smartphone sensors, allowing the phone to perform exceptionally well in low-light conditions. It provides a more detailed image and reduces noise, something that traditional smartphones often struggle with. This sensor is a glimpse into the future of smartphone cameras, where larger sensors improve image quality significantly.

4. Video Capabilities:

- **Cinematic Video Quality:** The **Realme Concept Phone** also emphasizes video production, offering **4K video recording** at 30fps and cinematic effects using the interchangeable lens system. This makes it an appealing option for mobile filmmakers, as they can now achieve **high-quality video** without needing heavy camera gear.

5. Portability and Affordability:

- Unlike DSLR or mirrorless systems that require bulky equipment and accessories, the **Realme Concept Phone** is compact and lightweight, making it ideal for travelers and content creators on the go. Its **affordability** compared to traditional cameras ensures that professional-level photography and videography are accessible to a wider audience.

8.4 Realme Concept vs Competitor Modular Camera Systems

The **Realme Concept Phone** is one of the first smartphones to introduce a **modular lens system**, offering a new level of flexibility and creativity for mobile photography. But how does it compare to other smartphones and competitor modular camera systems? Let's dive into how the **Realme Concept Phone** stacks up against other brands with similar features.

1. Realme Concept Phone vs. Xiaomi's Modular Camera (2022 Concept):

- **Realme Concept Phone:** The **Realme Concept Phone** stands out with its **interchangeable lens system** that supports multiple professional-grade lenses such as **portrait, telephoto,** and **wide-angle lenses.** This setup allows for more personalized control over photography styles, providing a DSLR-like experience in a mobile format.

- **Xiaomi Modular Camera:** Xiaomi introduced a similar modular camera system, but it was primarily focused on allowing users to attach a full-frame mirrorless lens system. While Xiaomi's approach is more focused on compatibility with **DSLR-style lenses,** Realme's system gives users a more streamlined experience, specifically designed for smartphone use with smaller, more portable lenses.

- **Comparison:** While both systems offer lens swapping, **Realme's system is more accessible** to the average smartphone user, while Xiaomi's modular camera offers more flexibility but might feel a bit more cumbersome, especially for casual shooters.

2. Realme Concept Phone vs. LG's Dual Camera System (V40 and V50 ThinQ):

- **Realme Concept Phone:** The **Realme Concept Phone** offers a **modular lens system,** allowing users to physically swap lenses for different types of shots. The **1-inch Sony sensor** in the phone allows for exceptional low-light performance and detail capture, making it ideal for both professional photographers and casual users.

- **LG Dual Camera System:** LG's **dual camera systems** focus on providing both a wide-angle and telephoto lens on the same phone. While this provides versatility, it still limits the user to the fixed lenses on the phone.

- **Comparison:** Realme's modular lens system provides **greater versatility** compared to LG's **dual camera systems.** The ability to swap out lenses offers more creative control, especially in specialized shots like macro or portrait photography.

3. Realme Concept Phone vs. Apple iPhone Pro Models:

- **Realme Concept Phone:** The **Realme Concept Phone** allows for complete flexibility with interchangeable lenses and a dedicated **Pro Mode** for manual control. This offers DSLR-like control, including adjustable aperture, shutter speed, and ISO, giving users more hands-on control over their shots.

- **Apple iPhone Pro Models:** Apple's **iPhone Pro models** have been leaders in mobile photography with excellent **multi-lens systems** (wide, ultra-wide, telephoto), but they don't allow for lens swapping. The iPhone's strength lies in **computational photography** with powerful **AI-enhancements** and excellent **color accuracy**.

- **Comparison:** While the **iPhone Pro** offers top-tier **AI features** and powerful **multi-lens setups**, **Realme's modular lens system** provides more versatility in terms of choosing lenses, giving it a **creative edge** for photographers looking to experiment with different styles and focal lengths.

4. Realme Concept Phone vs. Samsung Galaxy Z Fold with Modular Camera:

- **Realme Concept Phone:** The **Realme Concept Phone** excels with its **compact modular system** and high-performance sensor, allowing for a hybrid mobile-camera experience. Its flexibility and control, paired with a customizable lens system, make it a good fit for users who want high-quality images without bulky gear.

- **Samsung Galaxy Z Fold (Modular Camera Concept):** Samsung has also dabbled with modular designs, most notably in its **foldable phones.** While Samsung has offered some advanced camera setups, they typically focus on a **multi-lens array** and folding technology, rather than interchangeable lenses.

- **Comparison: Realme's modular system** offers more direct control over the lenses, allowing users to physically swap out lenses for different photographic needs. In contrast, Samsung's **modular foldables** prioritize **form factor** and overall flexibility rather than lens customization.

8.5 Is the Realme Concept Phone Right for You? A Quick Buyer's Guide

If you're considering the **Realme Concept Phone,** it's essential to evaluate whether this device is the right fit for your photography needs and general smartphone use. Here's a quick guide to help you determine if the **Realme Concept Phone** is the right choice for you.

1. Who Should Buy the Realme Concept Phone?

- **Photography Enthusiasts:** If you're someone who loves experimenting with different types of photography, the **Realme Concept Phone** is a great choice. The **modular lens system** lets you explore various styles, such as **portrait photography, landscape,** and **macro shots** with ease.

- **Mobile Creators and Vloggers:** The phone's ability to swap lenses and shoot in **4K video** makes it an excellent option for vloggers and content creators who need both quality video and the ability to change perspectives.

- **Travelers and Minimalist Photographers:** If you want a device that combines the power of a professional camera with the portability of a smartphone, the **Realme Concept Phone** is ideal. You won't have to carry around heavy camera equipment—just swap lenses and go.

- **Tech-Savvy Users:** The **Realme Concept Phone** is packed with **advanced features** like **manual controls, RAW photo capture,** and a **high-quality** sensor, making it an excellent choice for tech enthusiasts who want the latest in smartphone innovation.

2. Who Should Consider Other Options?

- **Casual Users or Basic Photographers:** If you're someone who takes occasional photos and prefers an automatic experience, the **Realme Concept Phone** may offer more features than you need. Phones like the **iPhone** or **Samsung Galaxy** might be more user-friendly if you don't plan to use manual controls regularly.

- **Those Who Don't Need Interchangeable Lenses:** If you don't require **lens swapping** and are satisfied with a standard multi-lens setup, the **Realme Concept Phone**'s unique lens system might be more of a novelty than a necessity. Devices like the **iPhone 14 Pro** or **Samsung Galaxy S23 Ultra** already offer excellent multi-lens systems.

- **Budget-Conscious Buyers:** While the **Realme Concept Phone** offers significant value for its advanced features, it may be priced higher than simpler smartphones. If you don't need the specialized lens system and other advanced features, more affordable phones may meet your needs.

3. Key Considerations:

- **Price:** Consider your budget. While the **Realme Concept Phone** offers great value for its capabilities, it's more expensive than many standard smartphones.

- **User Experience:** The phone's **manual controls** and **lens system** offer more creative freedom, but if you're used to **automatic** shooting modes, there may be a learning curve. The **Realme Concept Phone** is perfect for users who want hands-on control.

- **Longevity:** As the mobile photography landscape continues to evolve, consider how future software updates will enhance the **Realme Concept Phone's** features and compatibility with newer lenses.

Chapter 9

The Future of Photography with Realme

Realme has consistently demonstrated a commitment to advancing mobile photography, introducing innovative features that bridge the gap between smartphone convenience and professional-grade imaging. At the Mobile World Congress (MWC) 2025, Realme unveiled several groundbreaking concepts and features that shed light on its vision for the future of mobile photography.

Interchangeable-Lens Concept:

At MWC 2025, Realme introduced a prototype featuring a 1-inch custom Sony sensor paired with a unique lens mount system. This design allows users to attach DSLR lenses directly to the smartphone, aiming to deliver optical clarity and depth previously unattainable in mobile devices. Realme demonstrated this concept with a 73mm portrait lens and a 234mm 10x telephoto lens, highlighting its potential to revolutionize mobile photography.

AI-Powered Imaging Features:

Beyond hardware innovations, Realme is enhancing user experience through AI-driven software features. One such feature, the AI Voice-based Retoucher, enables users to edit photos using voice commands, simplifying tasks like background removal or sky color adjustments without manual intervention.

Realme 14 Pro Series Innovations:

The Realme 14 Pro Series introduces several notable features:

- **Triple Flash System:** A world-first triple flash system designed for night portraits, enhancing low-light photography by providing balanced and natural lighting.
- **Cold-Sensitive Color-Changing Technology:** This technology allows the phone's color to change in response to temperature variations, offering a dynamic and personalized aesthetic.

Looking Ahead:

Realme's recent innovations underscore a strategic focus on merging advanced hardware with intuitive software to push the boundaries of mobile photography. By integrating features traditionally reserved for professional cameras and enhancing them with AI capabilities, Realme is setting new standards for what users can expect from smartphone photography. As these concepts transition from prototypes to commercial products, they promise to offer users unprecedented creative control and imaging quality.

9.3 How Realme Continues to Push Boundaries in Smartphone Photography

Realme has consistently pushed the limits of mobile photography, aiming to deliver cutting-edge technology and features that elevate the smartphone camera experience. Here's how Realme continues to lead the way:

1. Transformable Lens System:

The **Realme Concept Phone** introduced the revolutionary **modular lens system,** allowing users to swap lenses like a traditional DSLR or mirrorless camera. This level of flexibility in a smartphone is unprecedented, enabling users to choose from various lenses, such as **portrait, telephoto,** and **wide-angle lenses,** for different photography scenarios. Realme's move into modular lenses sets the brand apart from competitors, making it possible for users to achieve professional-quality shots directly from their phones.

2. AI-Powered Enhancements:

Realme has integrated **AI-driven photography** features that improve image quality and make photography more accessible to all users. For example, **AI Scene Detection** automatically optimizes settings based on the subject or environment being captured, ensuring optimal exposure and focus. Additionally, Realme has introduced **AI-based post-processing tools** like the **Voice-based Retoucher**, allowing users to edit their photos with simple voice commands, making the editing process both easy and intuitive.

3. Cutting-Edge Sensor Technology:

Realme continues to push the boundaries of sensor technology, with the **1-inch Sony sensor** in the Realme Concept Phone providing enhanced low-light performance and higher dynamic range. The larger sensor size allows for clearer, more detailed images, even in challenging lighting conditions. This sensor improves not just still photography but also video, enabling users to capture cinematic shots in both daylight and low-light settings.

4. Professional-Level Control:

Realme has also implemented **Pro Mode** in its smartphones, offering advanced manual controls for both still photography and video. These features, such as **shutter speed, ISO, aperture adjustments,** and **focus**

control, allow photographers to have full control over their shots, much like they would with a professional camera. By integrating these features into a smartphone, Realme makes high-quality photography accessible to a broader audience.

Through constant innovation and a focus on both hardware and software, Realme continues to challenge the limits of what a smartphone can do in terms of photography, giving users more control, versatility, and professional-quality results.

9.4 Why Now is the Perfect Time to Embrace Realme's Revolutionary Camera

Now is the perfect time to embrace **Realme's revolutionary camera technology** for several reasons:

1. Advancements in Modular Lenses:

The **Realme Concept Phone's modular lens system** opens up a new world of possibilities for mobile photographers. For years, smartphone cameras have been limited to fixed lenses, but Realme has changed that by allowing users to swap lenses like professional photographers. This innovation allows for a range of creative options, making the **Realme Concept Phone** a true game-changer in the smartphone market.

2. Superior Sensor Technology:

Realme has consistently worked to improve **sensor technology**, with the **1-inch Sony sensor** now featured in the **Realme Concept Phone.** This larger sensor captures more light, resulting in clearer, more detailed images, even in low-light conditions. With advancements in sensor technology, Realme continues to offer features that are traditionally found in high-end cameras but packaged in a convenient, mobile device.

3. Accessibility of Professional-Grade Features:

Gone are the days when you needed a DSLR or mirrorless camera to achieve professional-level photos. Realme's integration of **Pro Mode, AI enhancements,** and **manual controls** into smartphones makes it easier than ever for anyone to take stunning, professional-quality photos without needing complex equipment. Whether you're a professional photographer or a hobbyist, Realme makes it possible to create beautiful photos with a device that fits in your pocket.

4. Affordable Innovation:

In the past, professional cameras with modular lens systems and advanced sensors came at a high price. However, **Realme's pricing strategy** allows users to experience these advanced features at a fraction of the cost of traditional cameras, making it an affordable option for both budding photographers and experienced creatives.

5. The Future of Photography:

Realme is at the forefront of **AI-driven mobile photography,** with features like **AI Scene Detection, night mode,** and **voice-based editing.** The **Realme Concept Phone** is just the beginning of what Realme is planning for the future, and as the technology continues to evolve, the possibilities for smartphone photography will only expand.

9.5 Your Photography Journey Begins Here: Taking the Next Step

If you've been inspired by the possibilities of the **Realme Concept Phone** and are ready to elevate your photography game, now is the time to take the next step. Here's how to begin your journey:

1. Start Experimenting with Lenses:

The **modular lens system** on the **Realme Concept Phone** offers a unique opportunity to experiment with different lenses. Start by attaching a **portrait lens** for beautiful subject isolation, or use the **telephoto lens** for capturing distant subjects with incredible detail. As you experiment with different lenses, you'll gain a deeper understanding of how each lens affects your compositions and learning new techniques.

2. Learn the Manual Controls:

Take full advantage of **Pro Mode** and explore manual controls such as **shutter speed, ISO, focus,** and **white balance.** These features provide greater creative control and allow you to experiment with different shooting techniques. Play around with long exposures, motion blur, and depth of field to develop your photography skills and create truly unique images.

3. Explore AI Features:

Let the **AI-powered features** enhance your photography. Experiment with **AI Scene Detection** to see how the phone optimizes settings for different environments. Use **AI portrait modes** to capture stunning, well-lit portraits. AI features like **night mode** and **HDR** will help you achieve beautiful results with minimal effort.

4. Start Editing and Refining:

Once you've captured your photos, it's time to bring them to life with editing. Use **Realme's built-in editing tools** or external software like **Adobe Lightroom** to fine-tune your photos. Adjust things like exposure, contrast, and color grading to create the perfect shot. Learning to edit is just as important as taking the shot, and it allows you to enhance your creative vision.

5. Share Your Work with the World:

As you improve your photography skills, start sharing your work with others. Join the **Realme photography community** on social media or participate in photography challenges to get feedback and exposure. The **Realme Concept Phone** gives you the tools to create stunning photos and videos, and sharing your work with others can inspire you to keep improving.

6. Keep Pushing Your Creative Boundaries:

Finally, keep pushing the boundaries of your creativity. Don't be afraid to try new techniques, experiment with different lenses, and take on new photography challenges. The **Realme Concept Phone** is more than just a camera; it's a tool that helps you unlock your creative potential. With its advanced features and endless possibilities, the phone is an ideal companion as you continue on your photography journey.

Your **photography journey** begins here with the **Realme Concept Phone.** With its cutting-edge camera system, modular lens capabilities, and powerful AI features, you have everything you need to take your photography to the next level. Start experimenting, learn the ropes, and share your creations with the world—you'll be amazed at what you can achieve with the right tools and the right mindset.

www.ingramcontent.com/pod-product-compliance
Lightning Source LLC
LaVergne TN
LVHW051344050326
832903LV00031B/3730